Stanton's Prehistoric Primer

Or,
AN ABC'S OF EXTINCT ANIMALS

STANTON F. FINK

Acknowledgments
and Dedication

To my father, in whose books I discovered my first monsters.

To Will Caligan, whose help and encouragement is one of the primary reasons for this coloring book's existence.

To Mariano Silvera, who should have had his own artbooks

To Doctor David Morafka, who helped teach me to be more picky with my information.

To my friends, who helped push me to make this.

Table of Contents

Introduction

The purpose of this coloring book series is to provide information on various prehistoric animals both profoundly famous and incredibly obscure to artists of all ages. Of course, there is a lot of material to work with, as animals have been a major component of Earth's ecosystems for at least 670 million years.

If you, or your inner and or outer child do not see your favorite prehistoric animal here, it may be eventually featured in another volume. Or, contact me to have it put into a later volume.

Glossary

- **Aquatic**- Living in water.
- **Arthropod**- Any member of the animal phylum Arthropoda, including trilobites, arachnids, crustaceans, insects, myriapods and their relatives. All arthropods have armor-like, jointed exoskeletons made of chitin-derived plates, sometimes reinforced with calcium carbonate, and jointed limbs.
- **Cambrian**- A period of time in the Paleozoic Era from 541 to 485 million years ago.
- **Carboniferous**- A period of time in the Paleozoic Era from 359 to 300 million years ago.
- **Cenozoic**- An era of time in the Phanerozoic Eon from 65 million years ago until now.
- **Chordate**- Any member of the animal phylum Chordata, including sea squirts, lancet fish, and vertebrates (such as lampreys, sharks, tuna, frogs, lizards, chickens, and people). All chordates have, at least at some point in their life cycle, a notochord, a long, flexible rod, usually made of cartilage, or, in the case of most vertebrates, cartilage and bone, running down the back from head to tail, directly beneath the neural tube.
- **Cnidarian**- Any member of the animal phylum Cnidaria, such as jellyfish, box jellies, Portuguese Man'o'war, sea anemones, coral and the parasitic myxozoans. Cnidarians are usually radially symmetrical, and have unique, venom-injecting stinging cells called "cnidocytes."
- **Cretaceous**- The last period of time in the Mesozoic Era, from 144 to 66 million years ago.
- **Devonian**- A period of time in the Paleozoic Era from 414 to 360 million years ago.
- **Ediacaran**- The last period of time in the Precambrian Eon from 635 to 542 million years ago.
- **Eocene**- A period of time in the Cenozoic Era from 55 to 33 million years ago.
- **Fauna**- In an ecological context, "fauna" refers to the animal components of an ecosystem.
- **Formation**- In a geological or paleontological context, a formation is a group of rock layers.
- **Gnathostome**- A gnathostome is any vertebrate chordate with a moveable jaw (or had an ancestor with one).
- **Holocene**- A period of time in the Cenozoic Era from 12,000 years ago until now.
- ***Incertae sedis***- A Latin phrase literally meaning "uncertain seat." *"Incertae sedis"* is a term in classification used to refer to a species or group whose relationships with related organisms are unclear or poorly defined.
- **Jurassic**- The second period of time in the Mesozoic Era, from 199 to 145 million years ago.
- **Mesozoic**- An era of time in the Phanerozoic Eon from 249 to 66 million years ago.
- **Miocene**- A period of time in the Cenozoic Era from 23 to 5 million years ago.

- **Mollusk**- Any member of the animal phylum Mollusca, including snails, clams, squid, octopuses, tusk shells and chitons. Most mollusks have a calcium carbonate shell, and a toothed, file-like tongue called a radula. All mollusks have a cape-like organ, the mantle, which usually secretes the shell, and houses breathing organs, and a nervous system.
- **Nekton**- Any aquatic animal that lives either entirely or almost entirely in the water column, and relies on its own swimming or propulsion abilities to keep and move itself in and around the water column. Anchovies, porpoises and ichthyosaurs are examples of nekton.
- **Neogene**- The second third of the Cenozoic Era, comprising of the Miocene and the Pliocene periods.
- **Oligocene**- A period of time in the Cenozoic Era from 33 to 23 million years ago.
- **Ordovician**- A period of time in the Paleozoic Era from 484 to 440 million years ago.
- **Paleocene**- A period of time in the Cenozoic Era from 65 to 55 million years ago.
- **Paleogene**- The first third of the Cenozoic Era, comprising of the Paleocene, Eocene, and Oligocene.
- **Paleozoic**- An era of time in the Phanerozoic Eon from 249 to 66 million years ago.
- **Permian**- The last period of time in the Paleozoic Era, the time of "The Great Dying," or most severe of all known extinction events, from 299 to 250 million years ago.
- **Pharynx**- A structure in the throat of many animals located directly behind the mouth or oral chamber. In vertebrates, it often houses breathing structures, like gills.
- **Plankton**- An organism that uses water currents and waterflow to as its primary means of transportation in the water column because it is either too small to move long distances by its own power, or lacks the ability to propel itself entirely. Sargassum seaweed and jellyfish are two varieties of plankton.
- **Pleistocene**- A period of time in the Cenozoic Era from 3 million years ago until 12 thousand years ago.
- **Pliocene**- A period of time in the Cenozoic Era from 5 to 3 million years ago.
- **Quaternary**- The last third of the Cenozoic Era, comprising of the Pleistocene and the Holocene periods.
- **Terrestrial**- Living on land.
- **Triassic**- The first period of time in the Mesozoic Era, from 249 to 200 million years ago.

A is for *Andrewsarchus mongoliensis*

Phylum	Chordata
Class	Mammalia
Order	? Artiodactyla
Family	*incertae sedis*
Size	Skull 83 centimeters in length, body probably as big or slightly bigger than a Kodiak bear
Time Period	Middle Eocene, 48 to 41 million years ago
Location	Irdin Manha Formation in Inner Mongolia, China

Comments

Andrewsarchus mongoliensis is known from a single skull discovered by Henry Fairfield Osborn Senior from Inner Mongolia, in China, and named in honor of Roy Chapman Andrews. The skull indicates that the original owner was a flesh-eating animal probably bigger than a Kodiak bear or polar bear, or at least bigger than a large water buffalo.

The identity of *A. mongoliensis* has long been debated. Its discoverer, Osborn, argued that it was a mesonychian, a group of carnivorous, hoof-toed ungulates closely related to the cloven-hoofed, or artiodactyl ungulates (including hippos, antelopes and whales). Recent studies suggest that it was not a mesonychian, but an artiodactyl closely related to the hippos, the extinct entelodonts and whales.

Other fossil animals have been misidentified as being either other examples of *Andrewsarchus*, or closely related to it. Below *A. mongoliensis* are three individuals of the mesonychian *Paratriisodon*, on a beach.

B is for *Brontosaurus excelsus*

Phylum	Chordata
clade	Dinosaurida
Order	Saurischia
Family	Diplodocidae
Size	22 meters long
Time Period	Kimmeridgian Epoch of the Late Jurassic Period, 155 to 152 million years ago
Location	Wyoming and Utah, United States of America
Comments	The Apatosaurid sauropods, especially *Brontosaurus*, have had a long, illustrious and rather sordid relationship with humans (at least the former's fossils). In 1879, Othniel Marsh attempted to get the better of his hated rival, Edward Cope by announcing the discovery of an almost complete skeleton of a giant dinosaur, which he named *Brontosaurus excelsus*, that was missing its skull. In 1903, one Elmer Riggs argued that the material of *Brontosaurus* was too similar to that of the closely related genus *Apatosaurus* to merit being a distinct genus. But, with an evocatively iconic name like "Brontosaurus," the public tends to insist on not getting that memo. In 2015, a group of scientists finally successfully resurrected *Brontosaurus* as a distinct genus. While the public rejoiced, other scientists criticized this as a hair-splitting convention made into a publicity stunt. *Brontosaurus excelsus* was the archetypical sauropod dinosaur, and, was a forest-dweller that, if we assume that it had teeth similar to the related *Diplodocus*, fed by stripping off leaves and conifer needles from tree branches by pulling the branches through their jaws.

<table>
<tr><td>C is for</td><td>Comarocystites punctuatus</td></tr>
</table>

Phylum	Echinodermata
Class	Paracrinoidea
Order	Brachiata
Family	Comarocystitidae
Size	Theca/body about 2 to 4 centimeters tall, maybe up to 7 or 8 centimeters tall with stalk and arms intact.
Time Period	Trentonian Epoch of the Middle Ordovician
Location	Ottowa Limestone, Ottowa, Ontario, Canada
Comments	

Comarocystites punctuatus is the best studied of a trio of paracrinoid echinoderm species that lived in shallow seas in what is now North America. *C. punctuatus* lived in what is now Ontario, Canada.

Paracrinoids are an extinct class of stalked echinoderms superficially similar to their distant relatives, the sea lilies. Unlike sea lilies, paracrinoids had comparatively larger, pear-shaped or egg-shaped bodies, termed the "theca" ("thecae" for plural), and did not have the five-fold symmetry seen in most other echinoderms. Like sea lilies, *C. punctuatus* and other paracrinoids were filter-feeders, grabbing food particles out of the water column with their arms. *C. punctuatus* had two arms, though, another species, the appropriately named *C. tribrachiatus*, had three.

D is for *Deiphon forbesi*

Phylum	Arthropoda
Class	Trilobita
Order	Phacopida
Family	Cheiruridae
Size	Up to 3 centimeters in length
Time Period	Wenlock epoch of the Middle Silurian, 433 million years ago
Location	In England, the Wenlock Limestone of Dudley and Wallsall, and the Wenlock Shale of Malvern Tunnel. Bohemia, and Sweden

Comments

Deiphon forbesi is a peculiar phacopid trilobite from Silurian Europe, discovered by French-turned-Czech paleontologist Joachim Barrande. Barrande named this fish-skeleton-esque creature after British naturalist, Edward Forbes, in order to commemorate their personal .

The glabellum is large, globular, and covered in wart-like tubercules. The pleurae, or side-extensions of the exoskeleton covering the legs, are modified into rib-like structures, and the cheeks are modified into long, recurved spines. The segments of the pygidium, too, are modified into long spines. The function(s) of these modifications are unknown, but have been speculated about for decades. A popular idea is that the the phishbone was a pelagic or planktonic swimmer that may have pursued prey in the water column. This idea falls apart when one understands that the rib-like spines would not aid in streamlining, and the round, warty glabellum would impair its hydrodynamics for swimming.

Most likely, it crawled along the seafloor, and hunted for prey, which it may have stored in its large glabellum.

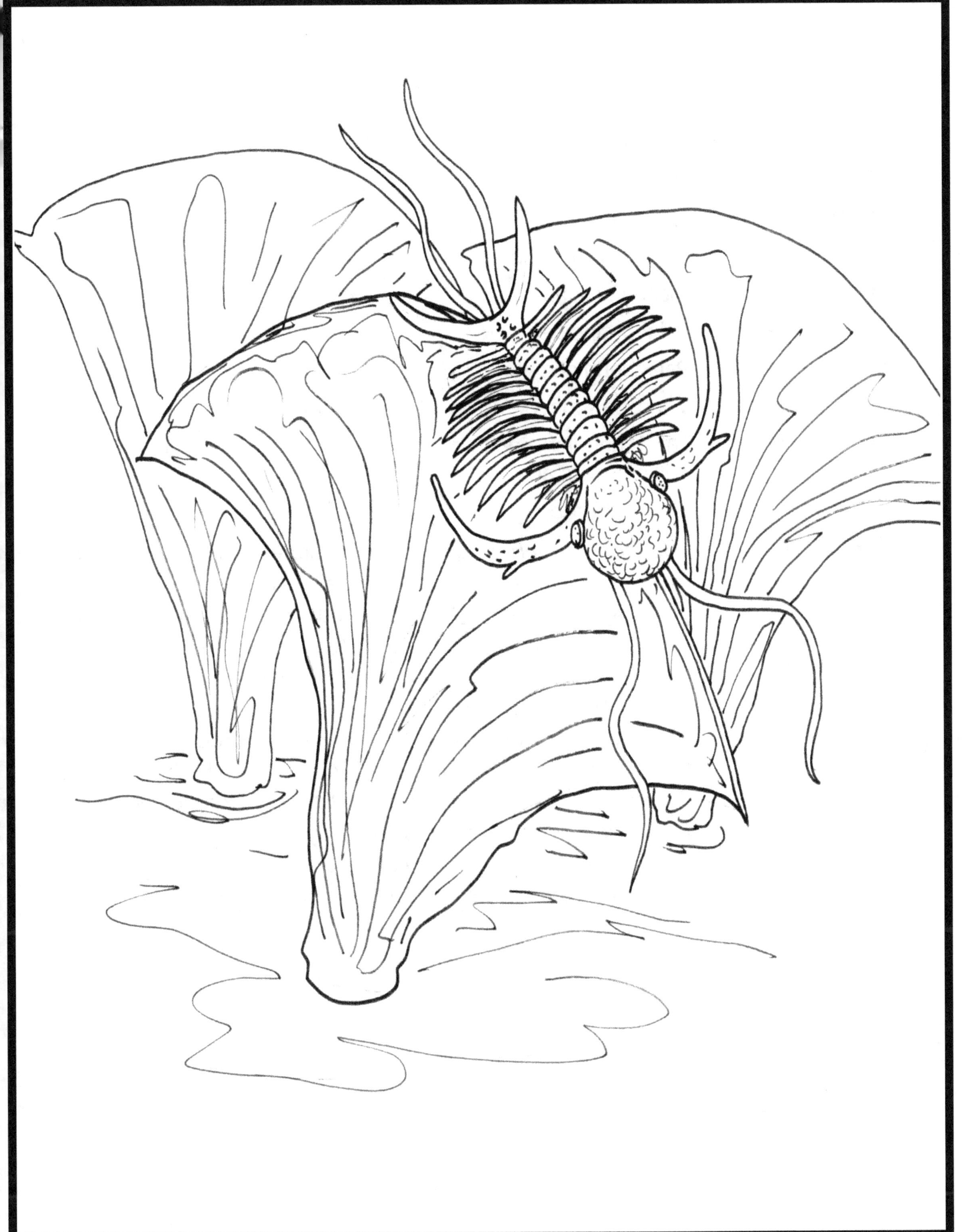

$\mathcal{E}$ is for *Eocicada lameeri*

Phylum	Arthropoda
Class	Insecta
Order	Hemiptera
Suborder	Auchenorrhyncha
Infraorder	Cicadomorpha
Superfamily	Palaeontinoidea
Family	Palaeontinidae
Size	Wingspan maybe up to 10 centimeters
Time Period	Late Tithonian Epoch of the Late Jurassic Period, 149 to 145 million years ago
Location	Central Europe
Comments	

Eocicada lameeri is an extinct hemipteran insect, or plant louse, from what is now Central Europe. It is known primarily from wings that detached from their owners after death, though, a few fossils feature whole individuals, suggesting a large (for a plant louse) insect with a wingspan of maybe 10 centimeters. *E. lameeri* cold be easily distinguished from the latter-appearing (true) cicadas by how its head was much much smaller. Whether or not *Eocicada* or its relatives in family Palaeontinidae could make noise like modern cicadas is currently unknown.

Like all plant lice, *E. lameeri* drank sap from plants. It remains unknown if it preferred a specific host plant or had several.

F is for *Foreyia maxkuhni*

Phylum Chordata

Class Sarcopterygii

Order Coelacanthiformes

Family Latimeriidae

Size About 190 millimeters long

Time Period Lower Ladinian Epoch of the Middle Triassic, 491 million years ago

Location Canton Ticino, Monte San Giorgio, Switzerland

Comments *Foreyia maxkuhi,* named for Peter Forey and Max Kuhn, respectively, is a strange, aberrant coelacanth from marine strata in what is now the mountains of southern Switzerland along the Italian border.

F. maxkuhni has a proportionally huge, rounded head with a low, horn-like point, a hooked maxilla and an underbite, possibly adaptations for being a slow-moving grazer of encrusting animals. The coelacanth bodyplan normalized during the Late Carboniferous, and would see few deviations afterwards, besides *Foreyia* and the fork-tailed *Rebellatrix*.

Despite its weird appearance, *Foreyia* is a relative of the modern coelacanth, *Latimeria*, and its closest relative is the plainer-looking *Ticinepomis*, whose fossils are found in the same strata and region.

<table>
<tr><td>G is for</td><td>Gemuendina stuertzi</td></tr>
</table>

Phylum	Chordata
Class	Placodermi
Order	Rhenanida
Family	Asterosteidae
Size	30 to 100 centimeters in length
Time Period	Emsian epoch of the Early Devonian period, 407 to 393 million years ago
Location	Gemünden municipality, Rhein-Hunsrück, Germany
Comments	

Gemuendina stuertzi is the best known and best-studied of the rhenanid placoderms, as it is the only rhenanid known from whole fossils. Because of the Gemünden rochen's beautifully preserved fossils, scientists know a great deal about its overall anatomy, to the point where *G. stuertzi* has become an iconic animal of the Devonian.

Fossils of *G. stuertzi* range from 30 to 100 centimeters in length: the largest specimen was originally described as its own species, "*Broilichthys heroldi.*"

Through *G. stuertzi's* whole-body fossils, rhenanid placoderms are understood to have had flattened bodies, long tails, and broad pectoral fins similar to skates and rays of today. However, even though rhenanids are often compared to skates and rays, because of the rhenanids' upturned mouths, they would have been ecologically more similar to modern-day goosefish and stargazers, snapping up any animal that wandered too closely to their mouths. Unlike all other known placoderms, the rhenanids' armor were made of a mosaic of unfused scales that correspond to the plates of other placoderms.

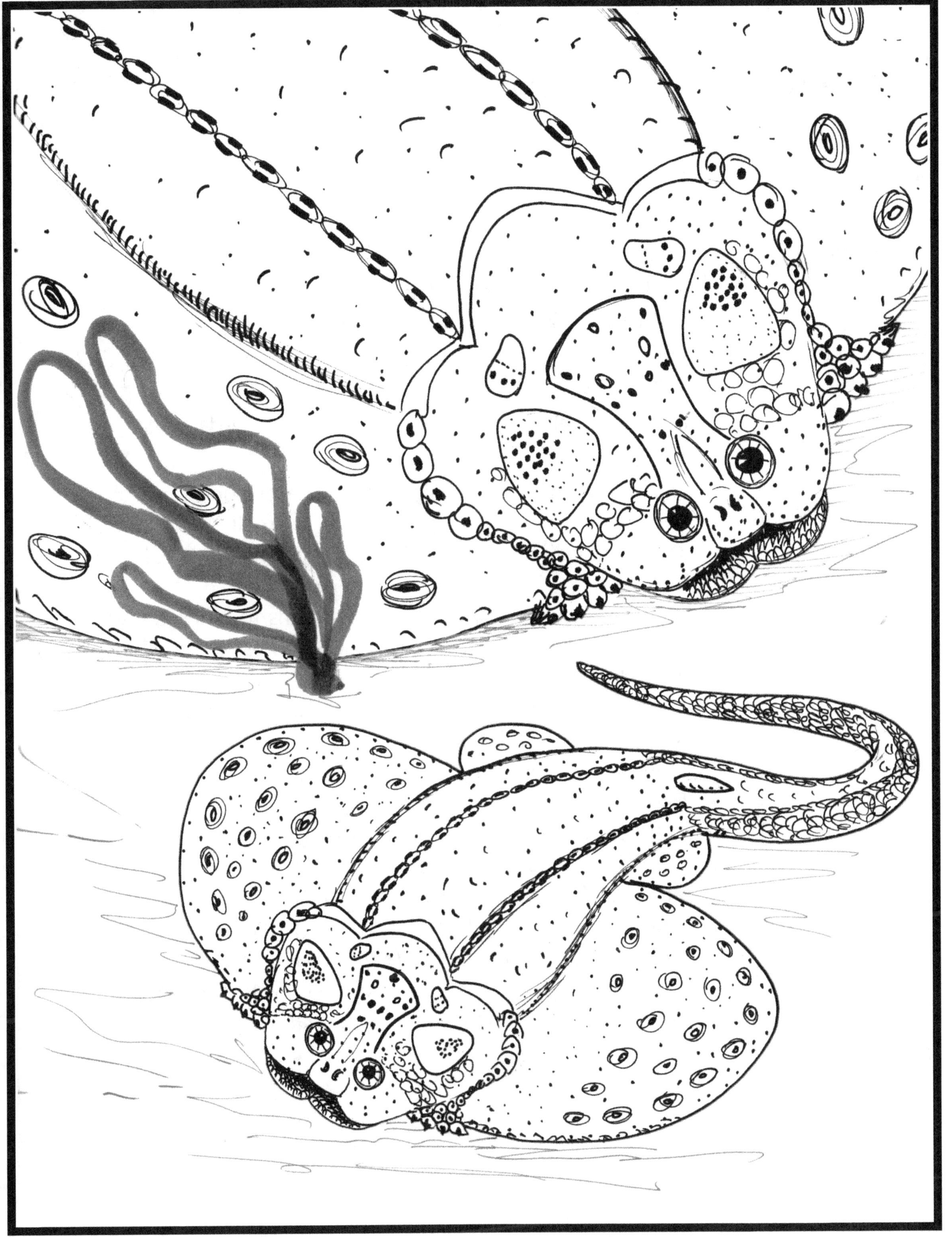

H is for *Hadrosteus rapax*

Phylum Chordata

Class Placodermi

Order Arthrodira

Family Hadrosteidae

Size Skull up to 16 centimeters long, living animal may have been 100 to 200 centimeters long

Time Period Late Frasnian epoch of the Late Devonian period, 372 million years ago

Location Kellwasserkalk of the *Manticoceras* Beds near Bad Wildungen, Germany

Comments

Hadrosteus rapax is a large arthrodire placoderm, probably about the size of a large trout or a small tuna, from the Kellwasserkalk of Bad Wildungen, in the state of Hesse, Germany.

H. rapax shows many similar adaptations to being a visually-based predator in an algae-dimmed sea seen in the unrelated arthrodire *Draconichthys*, including large eyes, and toothplates with fang-like serrations. In this regard, the panzerfisch and the Moroccan dragonfish can be seen as examples of parallel evolution.

Traditionally, the panzerfisch has been seen as a close relative of the terrorfishes of the genera *Dinichthys* and *Dunkleosteus*, and all three genera were housed within the family Dinichthyidae. However, with the recent restriction of Dinichthyidae to *Dinichthys* (and possibly the Chinese terrorfish, *Gannanichthys*), *Hadrosteus* has been placed in its own family, Hadrosteidae together with the mysterious Cleveland Famennian genus, *Diplognathus*.

I is for *Ischnacanthus gracilis*

Phylum	Chordata
Class	Acanthodii
Order	Ischnacanthiformes
Family	Ischnacanthidae
Size	Up to 2 meters in length
Time Period	Lochkovian to Pragian Epochs of the Early Devonian, from 419 to 410 million years ago
Location	Tillywhandland Quarry, Forfar, Scotland

Comments

Ischnacanthus gracilis is a very large acanthodian fish from the early Devonian of what is now Scotland. Very similar species are found in other parts of the world, and were once thought to be the same species or genus (i.e., of *Ischnacanthus*). However, those acanthodians originally identified as *I. gracilis*, or *Ischnacanthus sp.* outside of Forfar, Scotland, are now considered to be different species in distinct genera. The *Ischnacanthus* fossils at the "Man On The Moutain" site in the Canadian Northwest Territories were recently reexamined, and determined to be new genera due to differences in their teeth and skulls.

I. gracilis, itself, lived in a freshwater lake system that experienced frequent volcanic activity. It was one of the apex predators of the local ecosystems, living similarly to a modern pike or gar, seizing smaller fish with its sharp teeth. As with all other acanthodians, *I. gracilis'* dorsal, pectoral, anal and pelvic fins were supported by massive, ornamented spines.

J is for *Jawonya gurumal*

Phylum	Porifera
Class	Hexactinellida
clade	Heteractinida
Family	Wewokellidae
Size	About up to 3 centimeters in height.
Time Period	Series 2 to early Series 3 of the Cambrian, from about 516 to 507 million years ago
Location	Tindall Limestone, Katherine, Northern Territory, Australia.
Comments	*Jawonya gurumal* is a vase-shaped glass sponge that lived in a sponge-derived reef in what is now the Northern Territory of Australia. The generic name refers to the Jawoyn People, an indigenous group which lived in the Katherine Gorge for thousands of years.

In addition to its distinctive shape, *J. gurumal* has a distinctive open-lace pattern the double walls of its body, which becomes closed near the rim of the exhalant opening.

K is for *Kaibabvenator swiftae*

Phylum	Chordata
Class	Chondrichthyes
clade	Elasmobranchii
Order	Ctenacanthiformes
Family	*incertae sedis*
Size	Teeth up to 3 centimeters wide, living animal have have been maybe 5 to 8 meters long
Time Period	Late Kungurian or Leonardian Epoch of the Middle Permian, 270 million years ago.
Location	Kachina Microsite, lower Fossil Mountain Member of the Kaibab Formation, near Flagstaff, Arizona
Comments	*Kaibabvenator swiftae* is a giant ctenacanthiform shark from the Middle Permian of Arizona. It is known exclusively from small, multipronged teeth typical of ctenacanthiform sharks. Most ctenacanthiform sharks were very small, the largest whole-body fossils being up to one meter in length. However, when the teeth of *K. swiftae* are compared to those of a more typical member, such as those of *Ctenacanthus sp.*, the teeth of *K. swiftae* suggest an animal similar in size to a killer whale, or a great white shark.

K. swiftae was undoubtedly an apex predator, and undoubtedly preyed on smaller animals, such as the primitive sharks *Glikmanius* (upper smaller), and *Diablodontus* (lower smaller).

L is for *Liliaspis philipovae*

Phylum   Chordata

Class   Pteraspidomorphi

Subclass   Heterostraci

Order   Cyathaspidiformes

Family   Ariaspidae or Cyathaspidae

Size   Dorsal shield around 30 millimeters long. Living animal may have been up to 60 to 80 millimeters long.

Time Period   Middle Lochkovian Epoch of the Lower Devonian, about 415 million years ago.

Location   Northern Ural Mountains, Russia.

Comments   *Liliaspis philipovae* is a cyathaspid heterostracan agnathan from Lower Devonian-aged marine strata of the northern or polar region of the Ural Mountains in Russia. It is named in honor of the geologist L. I. Philipowa. *L. philipovae* had an underslung mouth, and thoracic armor with very distinctive, woodgrain-like ornamentation on the external surface. This ornamentation increased the surface area of its armor, and probably housed lots of sensory nerves.

L. philipovae lived with its similar-looking close relative, *Paraliliaspis*, and both are descended from Silurian-aged species of the Late Silurian to Early Devonian-aged genus *Anglaspis*. The plates of the thoracic armor of *Anglaspis* are separate pieces, which, in *Liliaspis* and *Paraliliaspis*, are fused together into a single unit, similar to how the plates of the related amphiaspids' thoracic armor are fused into a muff-like structure.

M is for *Maofelis cantonensis*

Phylum	Chordata
Class	Mammalia
Order	Carnivora
Suborder	Feliformia
Family	Nimravidae
Size	Skull about 19 centimeters long
Time Period	Early Priabonian Epoch of the Late Eocene, about 37 million years ago
Location	Youganwou Formation of Maoming Basin, Guandong Province, China
Comments	*Maofelis cantonensis* is the first Asian nimravid carnivoran known from a mostly complete skull (Asian nimravids, in contrast to the excellent fossil records in Europe and North America, are known mostly from teeth and fragments). *M. cantonensis* lived during near the start of the Late Eocene in what is now Guandong Province, China, near Guandong City. It is a basal nimravid more primitive than either *Nimravus,* or *Hoplophoneus.* *Maofelis* would have probably been about the size of a puma, but much stockier (if one goes by the physiques of other nimravids), and had prominent sabre-teeth (which give the nimravids their collective common name of "false sabre-teeth").

N is for   *Norasaphus monroeae*

Phylum	Arthropoda
Class	Trilobita
Order	Asaphida
Family	Asaphidae
Size	Up to 2 centimeters in length
Time Period	Arenig epoch of the Early Ordovician, around 471 million years ago
Location	Upper portion of the Nora Formation of the Georgina Basin, Queensland, near the border with the Northern Territory, Australia.
Comments	*Norasaphus monroeae* is an asaphid trilobite from the Early Ordovician of Queensland. Its fossils are found in the Nora Formation within the Georgina Basin, which sits the western reaches of Queensland that borders the Northern Territory. During the Early Ordovician, the region was a deep seabottom, filled with numerous trilobites, most species of which, including all of the species of *Norasaphus*, appear to be endemic.

N. monroeae's discoverer and describer, trilobite specialist Richard Fortey, named this beast after the famous, Hollywood glamorgirl, Marilyn Monroe. The trilobite's enlarged, wasp-waist shaped glabellum reminded him very strongly of the glamorgirl's famed hourglass figure.

O is for *Oraristrixbrea*

Phylum Chordata

Class Aves

Order Strigiformes

Family Strigidae

Size Larger than *Strix occidentalis,* maybe a little smaller than *Bubo virginianus*

Time Period Rancholabrean Epoch of the Pleistocene, 240,000 to 11,000 years ago.

Location La Brea Tar Pits, Los Angeles, California

Comments The Brea Owl, *Oraristrix brea*, is a medium-sized to large owl that lived in the mediterranean scrub of what is now Southern California during the Late Pleistocene. It was originally described as being a large member of the earless owl genus, *Strix,* that approached in size to some of the smaller eagle owls of *Bubo*. The legbones, the humerus in particular, are proportionally longer than either those of *Strix* or *Bubo*, especially when compared to the ratios of legbones to wingspan. This strongly suggests that the Brea Owl was a cursorial animal that walked along the ground like a seriema, but could still fly very well. Whether the Brea owl ran down prey like the seriema or simply spent a large amount of time on the ground remains unknown.

Here, the Brea owl (largest in the picture) is compared to some other extinct owls known from the La Brea Tar Pits, including Kurochkin's pygmy owl, *Glaucidium kurochkini* (to the right of the Brea owl), and *Asphaultoglaux cecileae,* (to the left of the Brea owl).

P is for *Portalia mira*

Phylum
incertae sedis

Size
Holotype and only known specimen about 100 millimeters long

Time Period
"Series 3" of the Middle Cambrian, 505 million years ago

Location
Burgess Shale, British Columba, Canada

Comments
Portalia mira, named after Portal Peak, a mountain just due north of the Burgess Shale, is a mysterious, tentacled creature known from a single fossil collected by Charles Walcott sometime before 1918. *P. mira*'s first official description by Walcott was published posthumously published in 1931, four years after his death in 1927. In Walcott's description, he thought it was some sort of creature similar to a sea cucumber, or holothurian echinoderm, his train of thought being the inspiration for this particular reconstruction. F. Madsen, in 1957, suggested it was (probably) a sponge, and not a holothurian.

In life, *P. mira* had a sausage-shaped main body with tentacle-like structures coming off of it. Some tentacles branch into smaller tentacles.

Q is for *Qianshanornis rapax*

Phylum	Chordata
Class	Aves
Order	Cariamae
Family	Qianshanornithidae
Size	Probably similar in size to a feral pigeon or a merlin falcon
Time Period	Late Selandian Epoch of the Paleocene, about 61 to 59 million years ago
Location	Upper Member of the Wanghudun Formation in Qianshan Basin, Anhui Province, China
Comments	

Qianshanornis rapax is an extinct, Chinese relative of the South American seriemas that lived in what is now Anhui Province of China. *Q. rapax* would have probably looked like a very small guan or seriema about the size of a pigeon or a large falconet.

The most interesting feature of *Q. rapax* is the enlarged, lengthened second toe (the middle toe), which had apparently been modified into a killing talon similar in function, if not form, to the killing claws of dromeosaur theropod dinosaurs.

Although only feet and legbones have been found, the dimensions of the joints suggest that the living animal was a competent flier, at least, much more than its closest relative, the mysterious, crake-like *Strigogyps* of Eocene Germany. It may have been that *Qianshanornis* searched for prey on a high perch, then flew down and pounced on a suitable victim, killing it by piercing with its enlarged talon.

R is for *Raphus cucullatus*

Phylum	Chordata
Class	Aves
Order	Columbiformes
Family	Columbidae
Subfamily	Raphinae
Size	Living animals were up to one meter tall, and weighed from 10 to 17 kilograms
Time Period	Last living dodo on Mauritius was seen in 1662
Location	Island of Mauritius in the Indian Ocean, off the eastern coast of Africa.

Comments

The dodo, *Raphus cucullatus*, is the largest known pigeon, though, this was not fully understood until the 19th and 20th Centuries, centuries after the dodo's extinction during the middle of the 17th Century.

The origins of the dodo, and the other raphid pigeon, the Solitaire, *Pezophaps solitaria*, are murky, though, DNA sequencing shows that their closest living relative is the Nicobar pigeon, *Caloenas nicobarica*. The last common ancestor of both raphids appeared between the Oligocene and the Miocene somewhere in Southern Asia. Sometime between the late Miocene and the Pleistocene, the ancestors of both birds would eventually **fly** to the islands of Mauritius and Rodriguez, where they would evolve into flightless forms.

The dodo was a very large bird, larger than a goose or swan, and had pigeon-gray-blue plumage, with tiny wings, and a knot of white, fluffy tail feathers. A painting suggests there were brown forms, and the confusion of the Reunion Island Solitaire suggess there were white forms, too.

The dodo lived in large groups that wandered the forests of Mauritius, eating fallen fruit, seeds and tender vegetation, shearing and crushing their food with their powerful bills and their stone-filled gizzards. In captivity, dodos were maligned as being greedy eaters that ate themselves into obesity; ornithologists now understand this was because they gorged themselves during the food-filled wet seasons in order to survive the famines of the dry seasons.

In a scene from the Mare aux Songe, when it was a lake and not a swamp, greater flamingoes, *Phoenicopterus roseus*, wander in the background. In the foreground is a saddle-backed tortoise, *Cylindraspis inepta*, which is attended to by a pair of raven-parrots, *Lophopsittacus mauritianus*, while a pair of dodos wander on and in front of the tortoise.

<table>
<tr><td>

S is for

</td><td>

Shringasaurus indicus

</td></tr>
</table>

Phylum	Chordata
Class	Reptilia
clade	Archosauromorpha
clade	Allokotosauria
Family	Azendohsauridae
Size	Estimated to be around 3 to 4 meters long
Time Period	Anisian epoch of the Middle Triassic Period, between 247 and 242 million years ago
Location	Denwa Formation, Madhya Pradesh State, India
Comments	

Shringasaurus indicus is a horned archosauromorph reptile from the middle Triassic of India. The blocky skull has a pair of large, curved horns that are thought to have been used in displays. The living animal would have been a chunky quadraped up to 3 to 4 meters long. The teeth, which are similar to the teeth of the poorly known Moroccan archosauromorph, *Azendohsaurus*, suggest *S. indicus* was an herbivore.

S. indicus, or, at least the area where the jumbled bones of the 7 or so known specimens were found, lived in a floodplain, possibly near a lake, with bushy vegetation and a diverse assemblage of animals.

$\mathcal{T}$ is for *Tamga hamulifera*

Phylum   Proarticulata

Class   *incertae sedis*

Size   3 to 5mm long

Time Period   Late Ediacaran of the Precambrian, 560 million years ago

Location   The White Sea, Russia

Comments   *Tamga hamulifera* is a tiny, freckle-sized proarticulatan organism that lived in a shallow sea that occupied what would eventually become the portion of Russia that, today, surrounds the White Sea.

The generic name comes from a Mongol-Turkish word meaning a "cattle brand," and refers to how the hook-like isomers form a star pattern, suggestive of a wax seal or a cattle brand. Even though the isomers form a star pattern, they also display the staggered symmetry seen in other proarticulatans, such as the proarticulatan *Onega stepanovi*, from what is now the Onega River.

The form of *T. hamulifera* is similar to the plates of the palaeoscolecids, a group of Early to Middle Paleozoic armored worms possibly related to the priapulids, leading some researchers to suggest that it may have been a palaeoscolecid. This hypothesis falls flat when one notices that the average body of *T. hamulifera* is profoundly smaller than the average palaeoscolecid plate, and that nothing about the fossils of this freckle-sized beast suggest they were mineralized like the way palaeoscolecid plates are.

T is for *Tamga hamulifera*

Phylum   Proarticulata

Class   *incertae sedis*

Size   3 to 5mm long

Time Period Late Ediacaran of the Precambrian, 560 million years ago

Location   The White Sea, Russia

Comments

Tamga hamulifera is a tiny, freckle-sized proarticulatan organism that lived in a shallow sea that occupied what would eventually become the portion of Russia that, today, surrounds the White Sea.

The generic name comes from a Mongol-Turkish word meaning a "cattle brand," and refers to how the hook-like isomers form a star pattern, suggestive of a wax seal or a cattle brand. Even though the isomers form a star pattern, they also display the staggered symmetry seen in other proarticulatans, such as the proarticulatan *Onega stepanovi,* from what is now the Onega River.

The form of *T. hamulifera* is similar to the plates of the palaeoscolecids, a group of Early to Middle Paleozoic armored worms possibly related to the priapulids, leading some researchers to suggest that it may have been a palaeoscolecid. This hypothesis falls flat when one notices that the average body of *T. hamulifera* is profoundly smaller than the average palaeoscolecid plate, and that nothing about the fossils of this freckle-sized beast suggest they were mineralized like the way palaeoscolecid plates are.

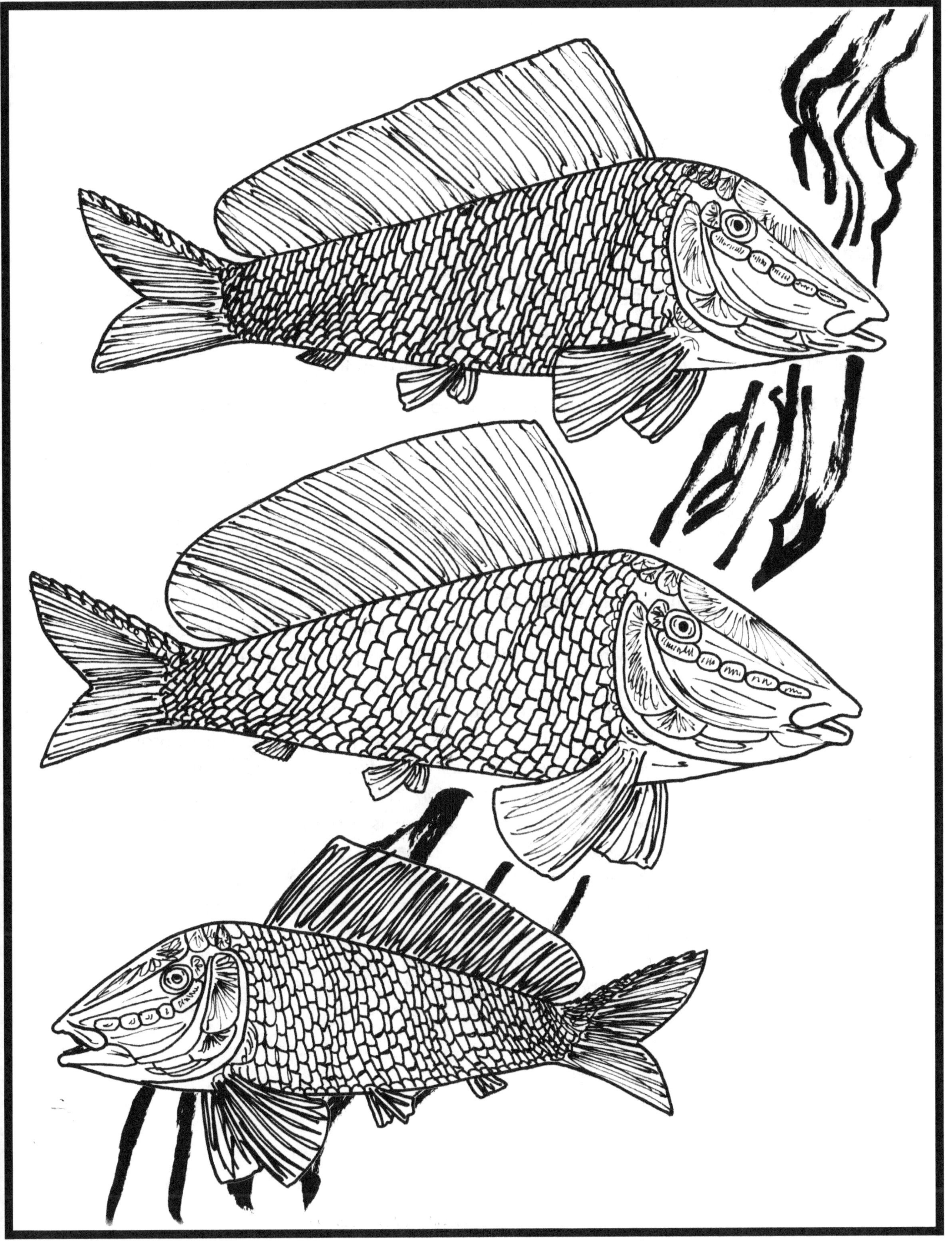

V is for *Vetulicola cuneata*

Phylum	Chordata
Subphylum	Vetulicolia
Class	Vetulicolida
Family	Vetulicolidae
Size	Average length of 9 centimeters
Time Period	"Stage 3" of the Cambrian Period, 515 million years ago
Location	Chengjiang County, Yunnan Province, China
Comments	

Vetulicola cuneata is the type species of the genus *Vetulicola,* and of the taxon Vetulicolia as a whole. This animal, which was similar in size to a large feeder goldfish, was originally described as a "bivalved crustacean," but, the articulation of the carapace was unlike anything seen in any arthropods. The posterior corner comes to a spine-like point, and the dorsal crest is large and recurved. The oral disk is stretched into a beak-like structure. The gill opens were diamond-shaped. The living animal would have resembled a wooden clog or a pointed shoe converted into an ice skate, with an oar-shaped tail emerging from the top of the heel.

A few specimens of *V. cuneata* (and, later, of the closely related *V. rectangulata*) were found to have small epibionts growing at the posterior end of the terminal tail segment, in very close proximity to the anus. These epibionts, identified as the putative, echinoderm-like entoproctan *Cotyledion tylodes*, lead some researchers to suggest that the wedgefaced was a burrowing organism, and that the epibionts settled on the exposed tail-tip. The nature of the fossils' burial, in addition to the anatomy of vetulicolians in general both strongly suggest against a burrowing lifestyle. A more parsimonious explanation is that the planktonic larvae of *C. tylodes* serendipitously attached to the tail-tips of vetulicolids, and survived into adulthood on a diet of their host's feces in a very thorough, "waste not, want not" commensal symbiosis.

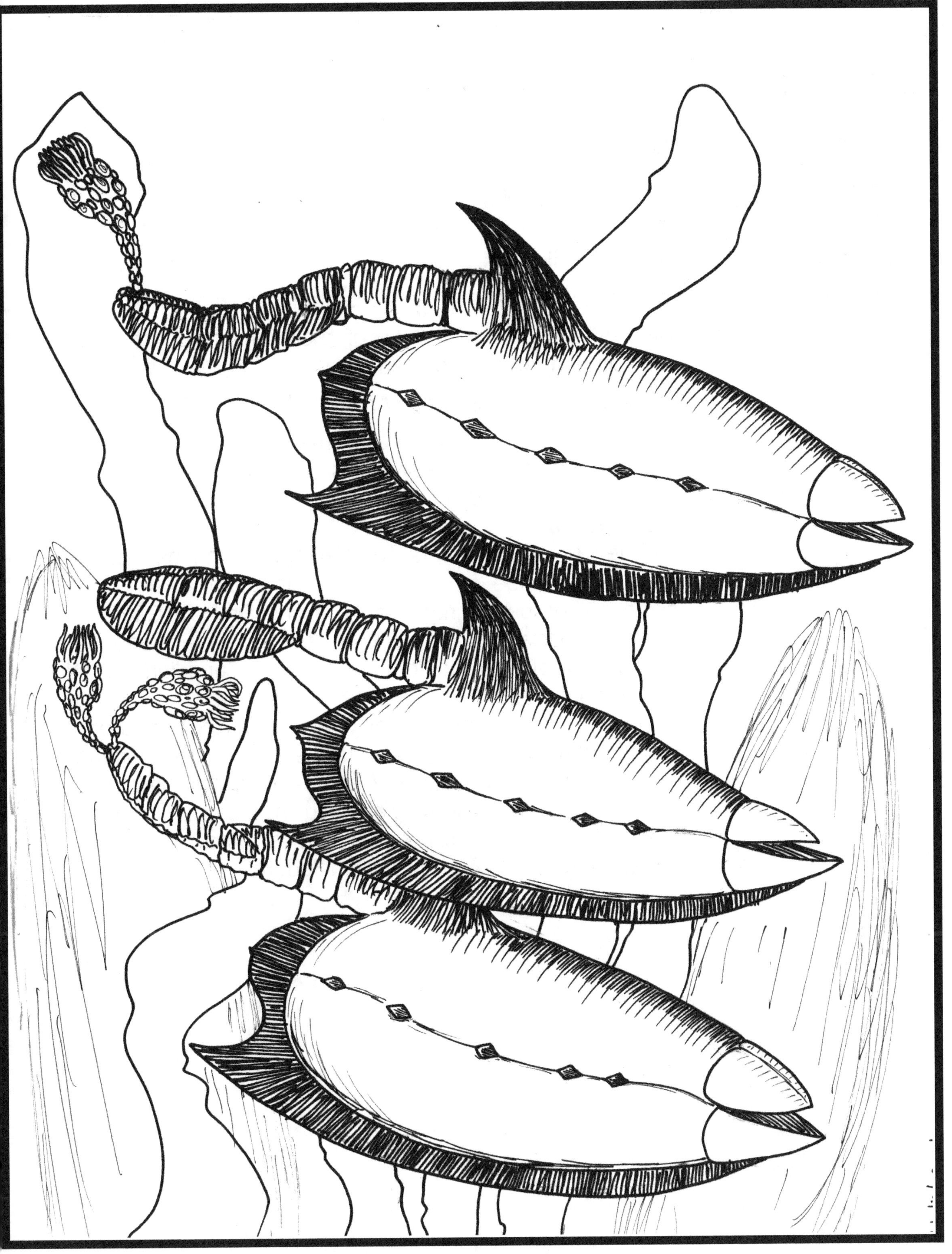

W is for *Wellingtonella gagnieri*

Phylum	Chordata
Class	Chondrichthyes
Order	*incertae sedis*
Family	Wellingtonellidae
Size	About 6 centimers long, and 2 centimeters wide
Time Period	Lower Sheinwoodian division of the Wenlock Epoch of the Early Silurian, 433 million years ago.
Location	Cornwallis Island, Canadian Arctic Archipelago, Canada.

Comments

Wellingtonella gagnieri is a primitive chondrichthyid, or cartilaginous fish, and represents what these animals were like soon after diverging from their ancestors, the acanthodians.

The generic name refers to Wellington Channel, on the northeastern side of Cornwallis Island, towards Devon Island. The specific name honors one Dr P. Y. Gagnier, a French specialist of acanthodians who lead an paleontological expedition to the Canadian Arctic Archipelago in 1994.

W. gagnieri looked very similar to a generalized acanthodian fish, though, it would have much smaller, less prominent scales. It lived in a deepwater environment that played host to a diverse ecosystem that held numerous species of thelodont agnathan fishes. Here, an individual of *W. gagnieri* attacks an *Archipelepis* thelodont.

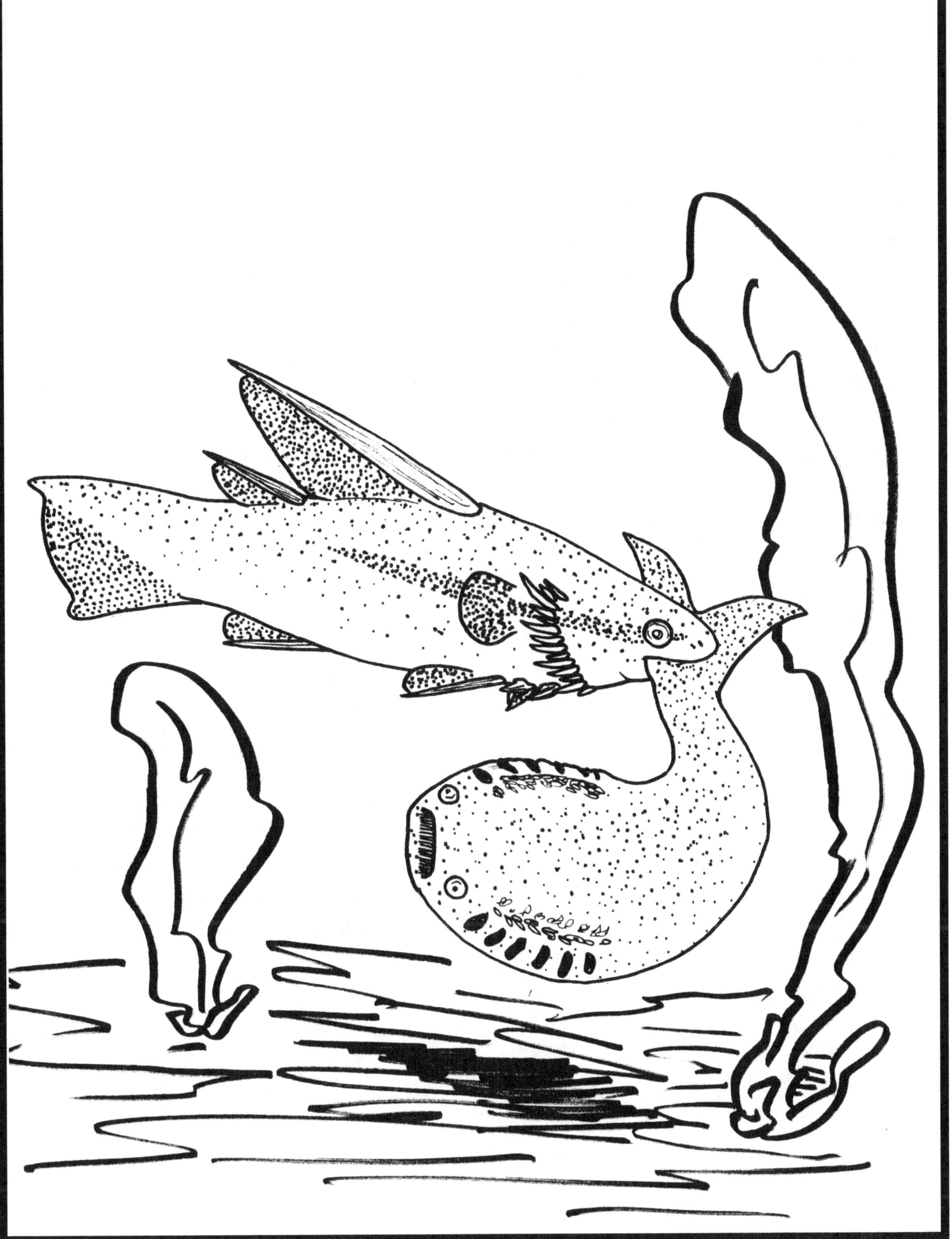

X is for *Xiangshuiosteus wui*

Phylum	Chordata
Class	Placodermi
Order	Arthrodira
Suborder	Brachythoraci
Family	?Dunkleosteidae
Size	Holotype and only known specimen suggests a skull at least 5 to 5.5 centimeters long.
Time Period	Late Emsian Epoch of the Early Devonian, about 397 million years ago.
Location	Near Xiangshui Valley, Jiucheng Formation, Wuding of Yunnan Province, China.
Comments	

Xiangshuiosteus wui is a peculiar arthrodire placoderm so far known only from a flattened skull roof reminiscent of a Buddhist cap. The generic name refers to Xiangshui Valley, "香水穀" near the region where the holotype specimen was found.

When the specimen was first studied in 1992, it was thought to be a transitional form between buchanosteids and coccosteids. A later study in 2013, however places the perfume trout in Dunkleosteidae as a close relative of the Australian Sea Boar, *Eastmanosteus calliaspis*, from the Late Frasnian-aged Gogo Reef, and no longer a transitional form.

The Late Emsian-aged Jiucheng Formation had an extensive community of placoderms, including several additional arthrodires and tiny antiarchs.

Y is for *Yantanglestes conexus*

Phylum Chordata

Class Mammalia

Order Mesonychia

Family Mesonychidae

Size Teeth and bone fragments suggest an animal about the size of a small fox or toy breed of dog.

Time Period Paleocene Period, 61 to 55 million years ago

Location Anhui Province and Guangdong Province, China.

Comments

Yantanglestes conexus (originally *Lestes* conexus) is the earliest known mesonychian mammal, found in Paleocene-aged strata in Anhui and Guangdong Provinces of China.

Y. conexus was a small, rainforest-dwelling, fox or weasel-like creature that preyed on any animal it could catch, like lizards, smaller mammals, or insects. Later species grew much larger, comparable in size to a wolf. Fossils of *Y. conexus* are not found association with other mesonychians, though later species of *Yantanglestes* are, including species from the genera *Dissacus* and *Hukuotherium*.

Mesonychians are an extinct group of carnivorous hoofed mammals long thought to be relatives of artiodactyls, or cloven-hoofed mammals and ancestors of whales. Now, though, mesonychians are thought to be related to artiodactyls, whales and odd-toed mammals, or perissodactyls. The ancestors of mesonychians, themselves, are unknown, though, it is assumed they evolved from some other primitive ungulate, or condylarth mammal group.

Z is for *Zhongjianichthys rostratus*

Phylum	Chordata
clade	Craniata
Family	Myllokunmingiidae
Size	Body length 2 to 3 centimeters: length of rostrum 1 to 1.2 millimeters long
Time Period	"Stage 3" of the Cambrian Period, 515 million years ago
Location	Chengjiang County, Yunnan Province, China
Comments	

Zhongjianichthys rostratus is one of the earliest known craniate chordates, and is one of several primitive chordates known from the late Early Cambrian Maotianshan Shale lagerstätte of Chengjiang County, China. Like the hagfish, *Z. rostratus* and other members of Myllokunmingiidae are not vertebrates, as their spinal chord is not a vertebratal column. *Z. rostratus* is an eel-like creature with a comparatively large nose that had nostrils equiped with nasal sacs. It had large eyes, and comparatively thick skin.

Here, an individual of *Z. rostratus* is compared to the largest known Cambrian chordate, *Yuyuanozoon*, a vetulicolian related to modern-day tunicates.

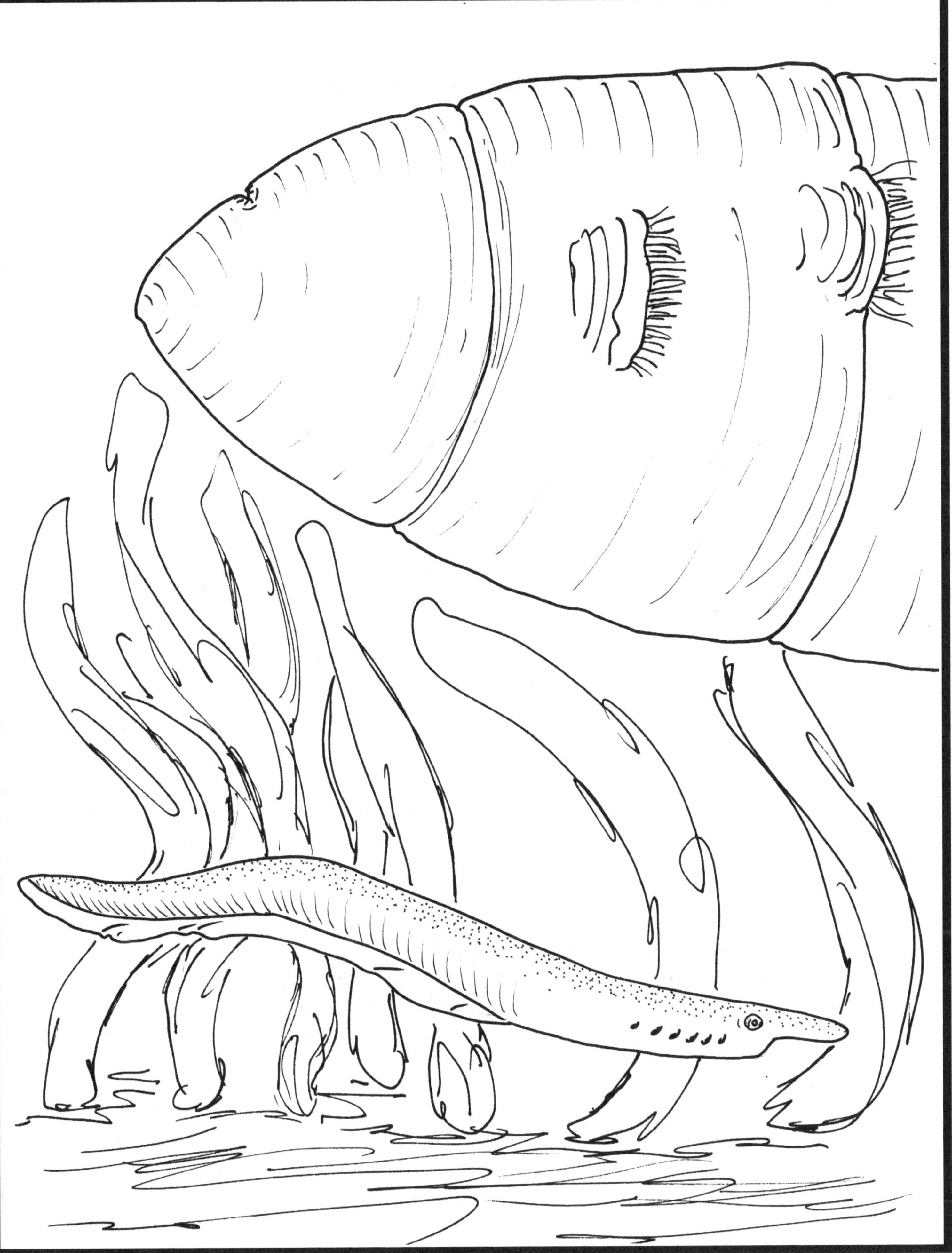

Bibliography

- Ailin, Chen, et al. "A new vetulicolian from the early Cambrian Chengjiang fauna in Yunnan of China." *Acta Geologica Sinica (English Edition)* 77.3 (2003): 281-287.
- Aldridge, Richard J., et al. "The systematics and phylogenetic relationships of vetulicolians." *Palaeontology* 50.1 (2007): 131-168.
- Averianov, Alexander, et al. "First nimravid skull from Asia." *Scientific reports* 6 (2016): 25812.
- Campbell Jr, Kenneth E., and Zbigniew M. Bochenski. "The Owls (Aves: Strigiformes) of Rancho La Brea." *La Brea and beyond: The paleontology of asphalt-preserved biotas, ed. JM Harris. Natural History Museum of Los Angeles County, Science Series* 42 (2015): 5-21.
- Cavin, Lionel, et al. "Heterochronic evolution explains novel body shape in a Triassic coelacanth from Switzerland." *Scientific Reports* 7.1 (2017): 13695.
- Cheke, Anthony, and Julian P. Hume. *Lost land of the Dodo: The ecological history of Mauritius, Réunion and Rodrigues*. Bloomsbury Publishing, 2010.
- Denison, Robert (1978). *Placodermi* Volume 2 of Handbook of Paleoichthyology. Stuttgart New York: Gustav Fischer Verlag. p. 105. ISBN 978-0-89574-027-4.
- Fortey, RICHARD A., and JOHN H. Shergold. "Early Ordovician trilobites, Nora Formation, central Australia." *Palaeontology* 27.2 (1984): 315-366.
- Fortey, Richard. *Trilobite: Eyewitness to Evolution*. Vintage, 2010.
- Hodnett, John-Paul M., et al. "Ctenacanthiform sharks from the Permian Kaibab Formation, northern Arizona." *Historical Biology* 24.4 (2012): 381-395.
- Ideker, Joe, and D. Yan. "Lestes (Mammalia) a junior homonym of Lestes (Zygoptera)." *Vertebrata PalAsiatica* 18 (1980): 138-141.
- Ivantsov, A. Yu. "Small Vendian transversely articulated fossils." *Paleontological Journal* 41.2 (2007): 113-122.
- Janvier, Philippe. "Early Vertebrates" Oxford, New York: Oxford University Press, 1998. ISBN 0-19-854047-7
- Kruse, Peter D. "Update on the northern Australian Cambrian sponges Rankenella, Jawonya and Wagima." *Alcheringa* 20.3 (1996): 161-178.
- Long, John A. <u>The Rise of Fishes: 500 Million Years of Evolution</u> Baltimore: The Johns Hopkins University Press, 1996. ISBN 0-8018-5438-5
- Long, John A. (1993). <u>Palaeozoic vertebrate biostratigraphy and biogeography</u>. 156: Johns Hopkins University Press, 1993. p. 369. ISBN 9780801847790.
- Madsen, F. Jensenius. "On Walcott's supposed Cambrian holothurians." *Journal of Paleontology* (1957): 281-282.
- Märss, Tiiu, Mark VH Wilson, and Raymond Thorsteinsson. "New thelodont (Agnatha) and possible chondrichthyan (Gnathostomata) taxa established in the Silurian and Lower Devonian of the Canadian Arctic Archipelago." *Proceedings of the Estonian Academy of Sciences, Geology*. Vol. 51. No. 2. Estonian Academy Publishers, 2002.

- Mayr, Gerald, et al. "A strigogyps-like bird from the middle Paleocene of China with an unusual grasping foot." *Journal of Vertebrate Paleontology* 33.4 (2013): 895-901.
- MISSIAEN, Pieter. "亚洲早古近纪哺乳动物生物年代学与生物地理学的新认识." (2011).
- MOORE, R.C. (ed.) 1959. Treatise on invertebrate paleontology. Part O. Arthopoda 1. (Geological Society of America and University of Kansas: Boulder and Lawrence). 560p
- Novitskaya, L. I. "Liliaspis-ein Poraspid aus dem Unterdevon von Ural und Einige Bemerkungen über die Phylogenie der Poraspiden." *Paleontographica A* 143 (1973): 25-34.
- Parsley, Ronald L. "Thecal morphology of the Ordovician paracrinoid Comarocystites (Echinodermata)." *Journal of Paleontology* (1978): 472-479.
- Rücklin, Martin. "First selenosteid placoderms from the eastern Anti-Atlas of Morocco; osteology, phylogeny and palaeogeographical implications." *Palaeontology* 54.1 (2011): 25-62.
- Sengupta, Saradee, Martín D. Ezcurra, and Saswati Bandyopadhyay. "A new horned and long-necked herbivorous stem-archosaur from the Middle Triassic of India." *Scientific Reports* 7.1 (2017): 8366.
- Shu, Degan. "A paleontological perspective of vertebrate origin." *Chinese Science Bulletin* 48.8 (2003): 725-735.
- Shu, Degan. "On the phylum Vetulicolia." *Chinese Science Bulletin* 50.20 (2005): 2342-2354.
- Szalay, Frederick S., and Stephen Jay Gould. "Asiatic Mesonychidae (Mammalia, Condylarthra). Bulletin of the AMNH; v. 132, article 2." (1966).
- Thewissen, Johannes GM, et al. "Skeletons of terrestrial cetaceans and the relationship of whales to artiodactyls." *Nature* 413.6853 (2001): 277-281.
- Tschopp, Emanuel, Octávio Mateus, and Roger BJ Benson. "A specimen-level phylogenetic analysis and taxonomic revision of Diplodocidae (Dinosauria, Sauropoda)." *PeerJ* 3 (2015): e857.
- Walcott, Charles Doolittle, and Charles Elmer Resser. *Addenda to descriptions of Burgess Shale fossils*. Vol. 85. No. 3. The Smithsonian Institution, 1931.
- Wang, Bo, et al. "Palaeontinidae (Insecta: Hemiptera: Cicadomorpha) from the Upper Jurassic Solnhofen Limestone of Germany and their phylogenetic significance." *Geological Magazine* 147.4 (2010): 570-580.
- Wang, Junqing (April 1992). "NEW DISCOVERY OF EARLY MIDDLE DEVONIAN BRACHY-THORACID (PLACODERM FISH) FROM WUDING REGION OF YUNNAN". *Vertebrata PalAsiatica*. **30** (2): 111–119.
- Wang, Junqing, and Zhu Min. "Age of the Jiucheng Formation of Wuding, Yunnan [J]." *JOURNAL OF STRATIGRAPHY* 1 (1995).
- Wang, Y. Q., et al. "A synopsis of Paleocene stratigraphy and vertebrate paleontology in the Qianshan Basin, Anhui, China." *Vert PalAsiat* 54.2 (2016): 89-120.
- Whittard, W. F. "LII.—A revision of the trilobite genera Deiphon and

Onycopyge." *Journal of Natural History* 14.83 (1934): 505-533.

- Zhu, You-An, and Min Zhu. "A redescription of *Kiangyousteus yohii* (Arthrodira: Eubrachythoraci) from the Middle Devonian of China, with remarks on the systematics of the Eubrachythoraci." Zoological Journal of the Linnean Society169.4 (2013): 798-819.

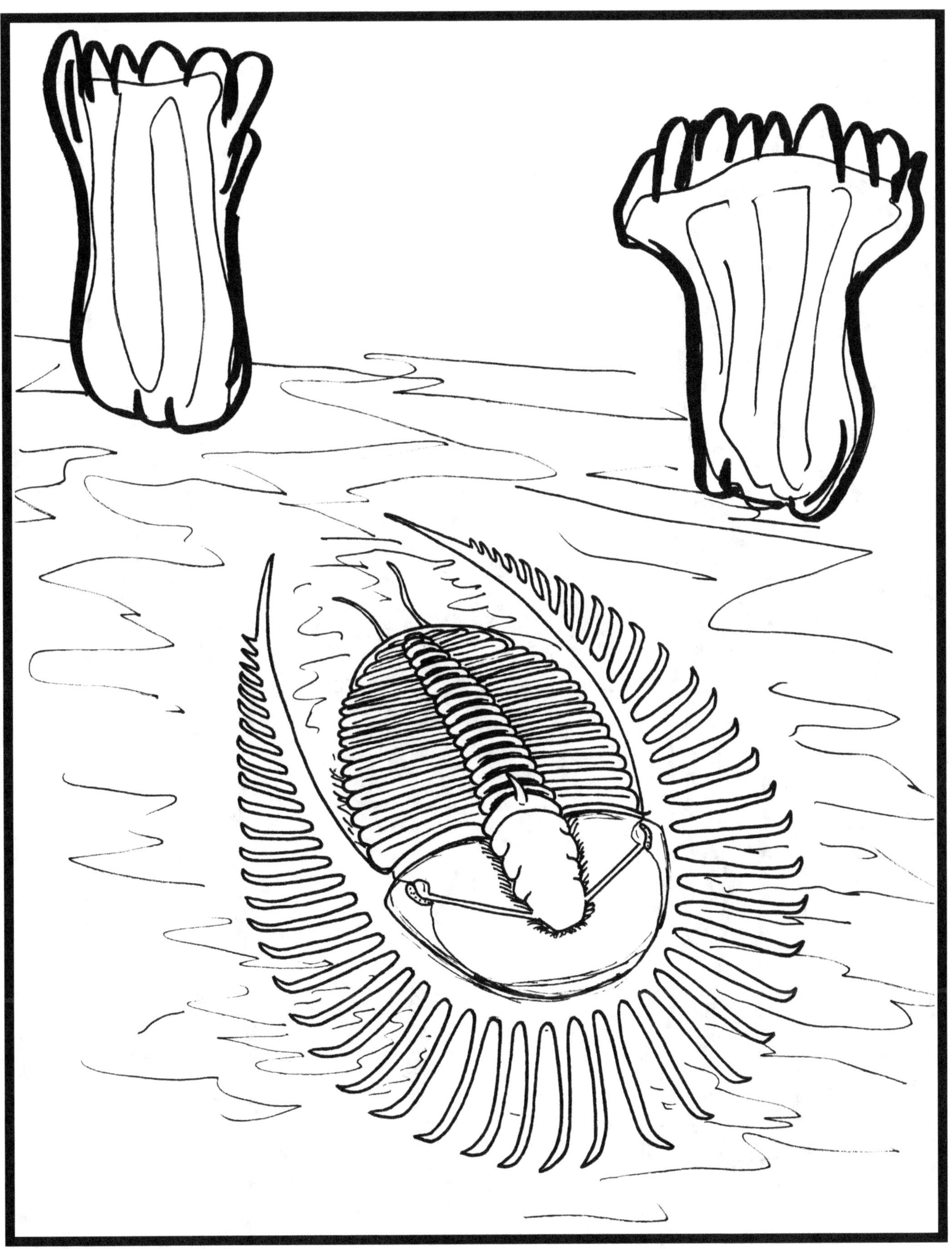

About the Artist

Stanton F. Fink is a student of Biology and Chinese Medicine, and makes a hobby of drawing monsters and researching flowers, arcane-looking creatures, prehistoric animals, fish, reptiles, birds and the occasional, really grotesque fungal fruiting body.

Stanton grew up and went to school in California and is currently living, drawing, and gardening in Oregon.

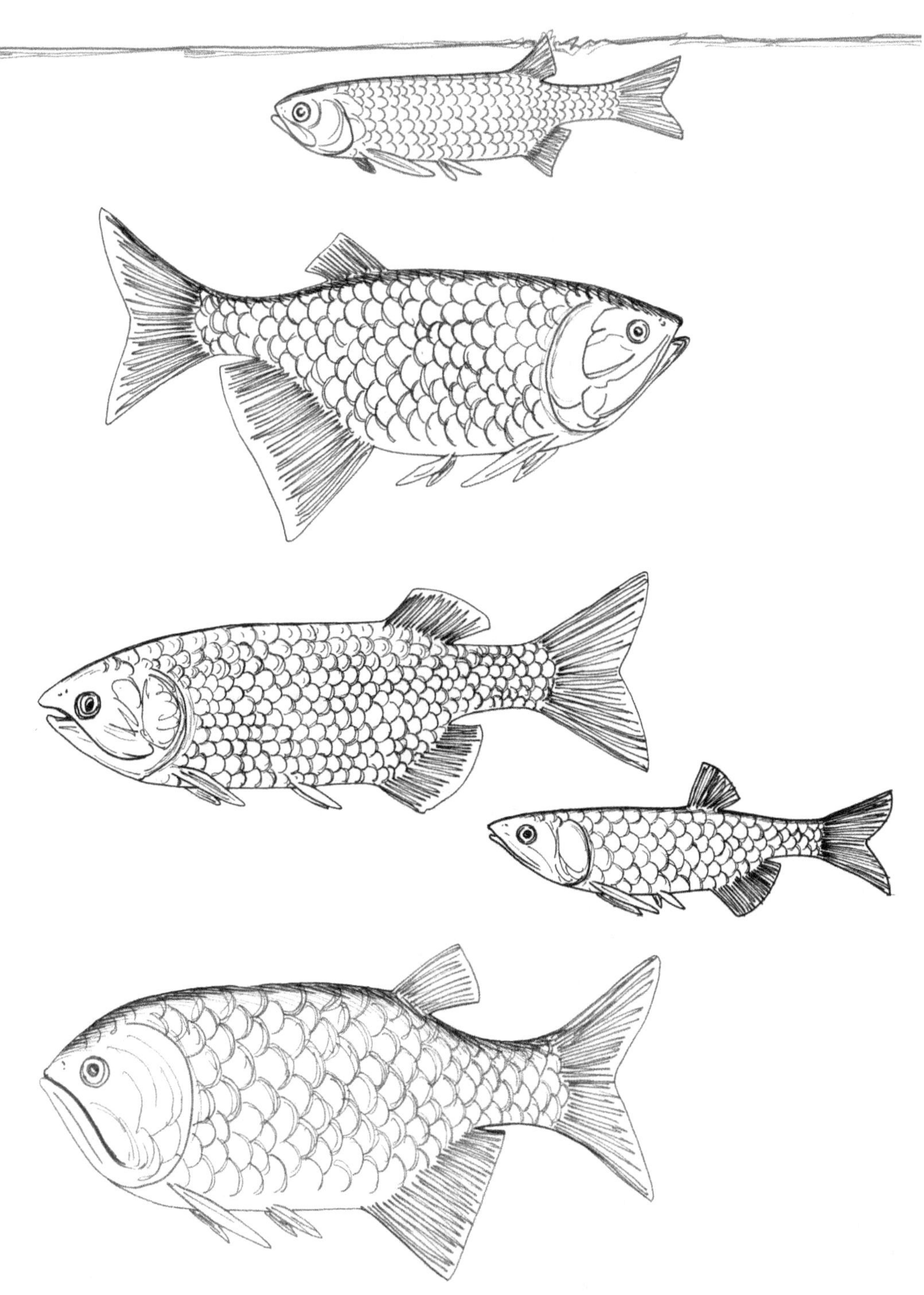